# Light and Shade

By Susanna Daniel

**CELEBRATION PRESS**
Pearson Learning Group

The following people from **Pearson Learning Group**
have contributed to the development of this product:

Joan Mazzeo, Dorothea Fox **Design** | **Editorial** Leslie Feierstone Barna, Cindy Kane
Christine Fleming **Marketing** | **Publishing Operations** Jennifer Van Der Heide
**Production** Laura Benford-Sullivan
**Content Area Consultants** Dr. Amy Rabb-Liu and Dr. Charles Liu

The following people from **DK** have
contributed to the development of this product:

**Art Director** Rachael Foster

Martin Wilson **Managing Art Editor** | **Managing Editor** Marie Greenwood
Jill Plank, Jane Tetzlaff **Design** | **Editorial** Louise Pritchard, Hannah Wilson
Diana Morris, Pernilla Pearce **Picture Research** | **Production** Gordana Simakovic
Richard Czapnik, Andy Smith **Cover Design** | **DTP** David McDonald
**Consultant** David Glover

**Dorling Kindersley would like to thank:** Rose Horridge in the DK Picture Library; Kath Northam for additional design work;
Johnny Pau for additional cover design work; and model Naadirah Qazi.

**Picture Credits:** Corbis: Roger Ressmeyer 27br, 29; Nik Wheeler 13cr. DK Images: Stephen Oliver 7bl; Science Museum 15br, 15bcr.
Galaxy Picture Library: 23cbl. Science Photo Library: Physics dept., Imperial College 19crb.

All other images: DK Dorling Kindersley © 2005. For further information see www.dkimages.com

For information regarding licensing and permissions, write to Rights and Permissions Department, Pearson Learning Group,
299 Jefferson Road, Parsippany, NJ 07054 USA or to Rights and Permissions Department, DK Publishing,
The Penguin Group (UK), 80 Strand, London WC2R 0RL.

Lexile is a U.S. registered trademark of MetaMetrics, Inc. All rights reserved.

ISBN: 0-7652-5234-1

Color reproduction by Colourscan, Singapore
Printed in the United States of America
5 6 7 8 9 10    08 07 06

1-800-321-3106
www.pearsonlearning.com

# Contents

# Introduction

Light is vitally important to our planet. Think about how often you use light. Maybe you turn on a lamp to get dressed, use sunlight to locate your bike outside, or click on a flashlight to find your socks under the bed.

Light is important for reasons other than seeing things. Without light, most living things couldn't survive. Plants need light to grow. They absorb light and use it to make food. Light from the Sun is the main source of heat and other forms of energy on Earth's surface. Sunlight also plays a major role in the changing seasons and the illumination of the Moon and planets.

Most animals and plants that live underwater need sunlight to survive.

Some of our sources of light are natural, such as sunlight. Others are artificial, such as electric lamps. However, all light has the same characteristics. Knowing what these characteristics are can help you predict how light will behave. It can also help you understand the role light plays in shaping the world.

The activities in this book can help you understand about light and how it can be manipulated in the creation of optical devices, such as a camera and a periscope. You will also observe the role of the Sun's light in shaping the cycles of day and night and the seasons and in illuminating the Moon's surface.

An electric lamp produces artificial light.

Before you begin each activity, gather all the materials you will need. Then use the photographs to help you follow the instructions.

⚠ If you see this symbol, please ask an adult to help you. Take your time working through each experiment, and have fun!

# The Behavior of Light

Light is a form of energy. When we talk about the behavior of light, we are talking about the way in which it travels and how it interacts with matter. For example, light behaves differently when it strikes a **transparent** object than it does when it strikes an **opaque** object. It will pass right through the transparent object, whereas it cannot pass through the opaque object. Light can be bent as it passes from air into water or glass, or it can be reflected, bouncing off the object it strikes. The activities in this chapter will show you some of the ways in which light behaves.

## Directing Light

You and a friend can direct light to see how it behaves as it travels.

### Materials

- scissors
- cardboard
- a hole punch
- a narrow-beam flashlight

### Procedure

**1** Cut three identical squares of cardboard. Then use the hole punch to make a hole in the center of each square.

**2** Line up the three squares so that the light from the flashlight shines through all three holes. (You may need a friend to help you hold the squares straight.)

**3** Move any square to one side or the other. Watch what happens to the light.

The Sun's rays show how light travels in a straight line.

## Transparent, Translucent, and Opaque

These photographs show how light behaves when it hits materials that are transparent, **translucent**, and opaque. The orange arrows represent **light rays**.

**1.** The rays go through the transparent material.

**2.** Some of the light passes through the translucent material, but some bounces off the surface of the material and scatters.

**3.** Light rays cannot pass through opaque material.

**1.**

**2.**

**3.**

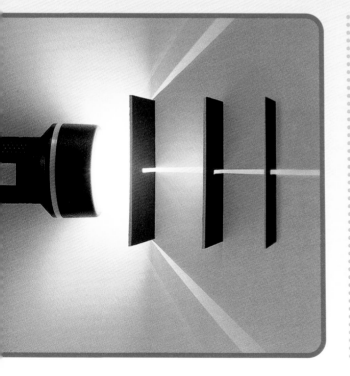

## Look and Discover

• **What happened when you moved one of the cardboard squares?**

Cardboard is opaque, and light cannot pass through it. However, light can pass through a hole. When the holes in the cardboard squares were lined up, light from the flashlight passed through them all. When one of the squares was moved, the light was blocked. This experiment shows that light beams travel in straight lines called rays.

# Reflecting Light

Sometimes light rays bounce off material that they encounter. This is called **reflection**. The angle at which the light hits a reflective surface affects both the way it bounces and how much it bounces. See for yourself how angles affect reflection.

## Materials
- a shallow black pan
- water
- a flashlight

## Procedure

1 Fill the black pan almost to the brim with water.

2 Darken the room. Then turn on the flashlight and hold it above the water so the light hits the water's surface from directly above.

## How Reflection Works

If you drop a ball straight down, it hits the ground and bounces straight back up. If you throw it at an angle, it bounces away at the same angle. Light rays work in the same way. Light rays are reflected from a surface at the same angle at which they hit the surface.

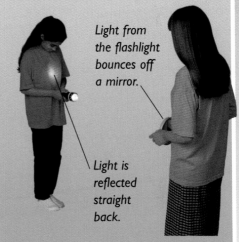

*Light from the flashlight bounces off a mirror.*

*Light is reflected straight back.*

**3** Shine the flashlight at a low angle across the water's surface.

## Look and Discover

- What happened when you directed the flashlight beam directly above the surface of the water? Did the water seem very dark? How much light was reflected back into the room?
- Compare that to what happened when you shined the flashlight at a low angle. How much light was reflected into the room? Which flashlight position reflected more light into the room?

When light strikes water from directly above, the water seems very dark. The light passes through the surface of the water and falls onto the base of the pan. However, when light hits water at a low angle, it is reflected back into the room.

9

# Refracting Light

When light rays pass from one transparent substance to another, they change direction. This is called **refraction**. This activity will help you explore how light refracts.

⚠️ **Ask an adult to help you with Step 2.**

## Materials
- a cardboard shoebox
- a pen
- a ruler
- scissors
- a sheet of white paper
- a glass jar
- water
- a flashlight

## Procedure

**1** Draw two vertical lines, about 1 inch apart, down the middle of one short end of the shoebox.

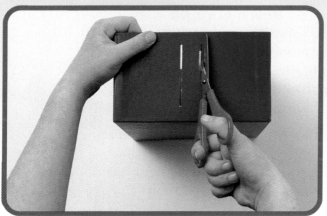

**2** Cut narrow slits along both lines with the scissors, leaving at least 1 inch uncut at the top and at the bottom.

**3** Cut a white sheet of paper so that it fits in the shoebox. Place the paper in the bottom of the box so that it lies flat.

**4** Fill the jar with water and set it carefully in the box. Line it up with the two slits.

**5** Darken the room. Then shine the flashlight through the two slits in the box.

*Two beams of light come through the slits in the box.*

## Look and Discover

• **Does each ray continue in a straight line inside the jar? Where do the light rays first change direction? Do the rays bend again as they leave the jar?**

Light passes through different substances at different speeds. When the light rays go from air into water, they slow down and refract, or change direction. The rays bend again as they leave the jar. The light is very bright where the rays cross.

11

# Making a Rainbow

White light, including sunlight, is actually made up of a rainbow of colored light. Create your own rainbow to see for yourself.

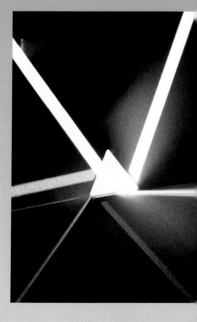

## Materials
- a shallow glass baking dish
- a hand mirror
- modeling clay
- water
- a flashlight
- a large sheet of white cardboard

## Procedure

**1** Place the mirror in the dish at an angle of about 45 degrees. Use modeling clay to secure it so it does not slip. Fill the dish halfway with water.

**2** Shine the flashlight onto the section of the mirror that is under the water.

12

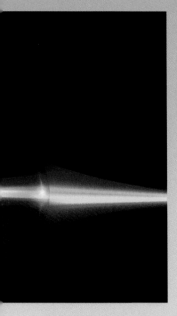

A prism separates white light into different wavelengths, so all the colors of the visible spectrum can be seen.

## Rainbows

Why do you sometimes see a rainbow during a rain shower? Raindrops act like tiny **prisms**. Light with longer **wavelengths**, such as red, is refracted less than light with shorter wavelengths, such as blue. As sunlight is refracted, the colors that make up the light are separated.

*A rainbow appears on the cardboard.*

**3** Hold the cardboard at an angle above the dish to catch the reflection of the light. Move the flashlight slightly for a better image.

## Look and Discover

- **What colors make up white light?**

White light is made up of different colors of light, each having its own wavelength. The range of colors, from red to violet, is called the **visible spectrum**. Some materials, such as glass, water, and objects, such as prisms, refract white light in such a way that the light separates into the colors of the visible spectrum. In this activity, the water produced a visible spectrum, or rainbow.

13

# Optical Technology

The study of light and its behavior has led to the development of many inventions, such as the camera and the **spectroscope**. The activities in this chapter will enable you to create simple versions of some of these inventions.

## Making a Pinhole Camera

You can make a simple camera to show how an image can be formed on a screen. The screen represents the film used in a camera to record the image.

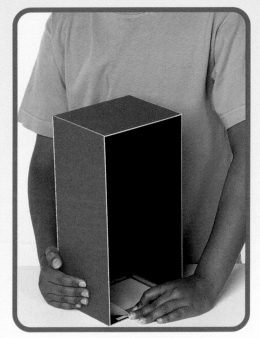

⚠ **Ask an adult to help you with Steps 1 and 2.**

### Materials
- a shoebox with lid
- matte black paper
- glue
- a pencil
- a ruler
- scissors
- tracing paper
- double-sided tape
- a drawing compass
- a 3-inch square of aluminum foil
- a pin

### Procedure

1  Line the inside of the shoebox with black paper. At one short end, cut out a square, leaving a 1-inch frame. Cut tracing paper to fit over the frame, and tape it in place.

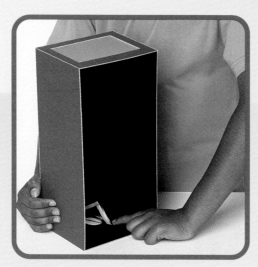

**2** Use the compass to draw a circle 1¼ inches in diameter at the opposite end of the box. Cut out the circle and tape foil over the hole. Poke a tiny hole in its center with a pin. Put the lid on the box.

**3** Stand by an open window in a darkened room. Point the pinhole at an object outside, such as a tree. Observe the image of the object on the tracing-paper screen.

## Look and Discover

• **What did you see on the tracing paper?**

Some of the light reflecting from the object passes through the pinhole and hits the screen. An image of the object is formed on the screen. The light beams cross as they pass through the pinhole. Light from the top of the object strikes the bottom of the screen, and light from the bottom of the object strikes the top of the screen. This makes the image on the screen appear upside-down.

## How a Box Camera Works

Light passes through the lens of a single-lens reflex camera and is reflected by a mirror inside the camera onto a screen upside-down. A prism in the camera sends light from the reflection out of the viewfinder to your eye right-side up. When you take the photograph, the mirror flips upward so that the light reaches the film.

William Fox Talbot made this box camera in 1835.

*image reflected upside-down on screen*

*lens*

# Making a Periscope

A **periscope** is an instrument used to view objects that may be hidden by some obstacle. Periscopes can be used to look around corners. In this activity, you will make a simple periscope.

Ask an adult to help you with Steps 2, 3, and 5.

## Materials
- a cardboard milk or juice carton
- a triangular piece of cardboard
- a pen
- scissors
- 2 small mirrors
- a pencil

## Procedure

**1** Use the triangular piece of cardboard to help you draw two diagonal lines on one side of the cardboard carton.

**2** Cut a slit along each line. The slits should be just wide enough to hold the mirrors firmly.

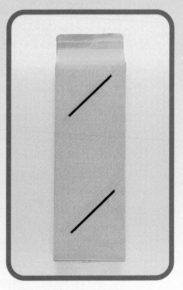

**3** Draw two lines on the side of the carton directly opposite the first slits. Cut slits as before.

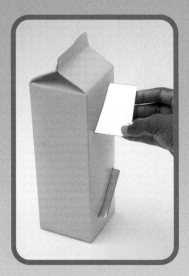

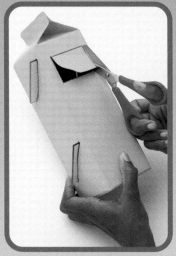

**4** Push the mirrors through the slits. Put the top mirror shiny side down and the lower mirror shiny side up.

**5** Draw a large square on the carton in front of the top mirror. Carefully cut out the square.

## Look and Discover

- What did you see when you looked through your periscope?
- How does a periscope work?

The object in front of the large square was visible when viewed through the periscope. In a simple periscope, light reflected from the object enters the square hole and strikes the top mirror. The top mirror reflects an image of the object to the bottom mirror, which reflects the image through the small hole to the observer's eye. More complex periscopes also use lenses to magnify the image.

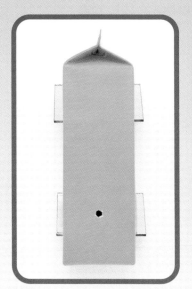

**6** Use a pencil to make a small hole in the back of the carton, level with the bottom mirror.

**7** Point the large square hole toward an object and look into the small hole to see around corners.

# Making a Spectroscope

A spectroscope is an instrument that creates a spectrum from a beam of light. It allows you to see all of the colors that make up that beam of light. In this activity, you will make a simple spectroscope and view the spectrums produced by a candle and by a glowing light bulb.

**!**
**Ask an adult to help you with Steps 1 and 2.**

## Materials

- thick cardboard
- a ruler
- a pencil
- scissors
- a sheet of dark paper
- tape
- a large sheet of white cardboard
- a candle and holder
- a magnifying glass
- a prism
- a lamp with no shade

## Procedure

**1** Cut out a 6-inch by 1-inch strip from the thick cardboard, cutting from the middle of one of the edges. Cover most of the missing section with dark paper, leaving only a 1/16-inch slit uncovered along its length. Tape the dark paper in place. Darken the room.

**2** Tape the cardboard to your tabletop with the slit at the bottom. Place the white cardboard about 20 inches away to act as a screen. Ask an adult to light the candle and place it behind the slit. Then have the adult or a friend hold a magnifying glass between the slit and the screen, moving it backward and forward to focus the image of the light onto the screen. If necessary, adjust the angle of the screen.

**3** Hold the prism between the magnifying glass and the screen. Rotate the prism until you see a spectrum. If the spectrum on the screen is too dim to show the colors clearly, try looking at the light source through the prism and moving your head from side to side until you see the spectrum clearly.

**4** Read the "Exploring Spectrums" portion of the activity. Predict whether the spectrum produced by a glowing light bulb will be similar to or different from the spectrum produced by a burning candle. Repeat the experiment using the light bulb as a light source.

## Exploring Spectrums

Different light sources produce different spectrums. An **incandescent** light source, one that is produced by heat energy, has a continuous spectrum in which all visible colors are present. Some gases produce a spectrum with a few brightly colored lines. Sodium gas, which is often used in street lights, produces a spectrum with a bright yellow line.

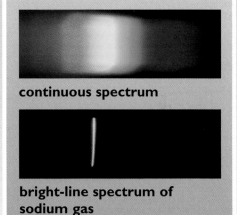

**continuous spectrum**

**bright-line spectrum of sodium gas**

## Look and Discover

- When you looked at the spectrum produced by light from the candle, how many colors could you see? Was the spectrum continuous, with no separate bright lines present?
- How did this spectrum compare with the one produced by light from a bulb?

Light from each source passed through the small slit, and the image of the slit was focused on the screen by the magnifying glass. When passed through the prism, the light rays were separated into a spectrum. Both light sources are incandescent, and each should therefore produce a continuous spectrum.

# Sunlight

Today we know that Earth rotates on its **axis** and revolves around the Sun. However, when the Polish astronomer Nicolaus Copernicus proposed this theory in the 1500s, most people refused to believe it. They were convinced that Earth was at the center of the universe! Luckily, a few bold thinkers, including Galileo Galilei, saw the wisdom of Copernicus's theory. As you do the activities in this chapter, you will follow in the footsteps of those early scientists who drew their conclusions based on careful observations.

## Day and Night

What causes day and night? Investigate with the following activity.

⚠️ **Ask an adult to help you with Step 1.**

### Materials
- a plastic foam ball
- a thin wooden skewer about 10 inches long
- a felt-tip pen
- modeling clay
- a desk lamp

### Procedure

1 Ask an adult to help you carefully push the wooden skewer through the center of the plastic foam ball. Use a felt-tip pen to make a line of large dots around the middle of the ball, as shown above.

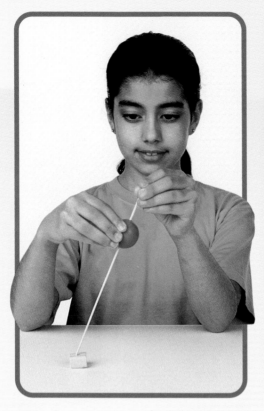

**2** Secure one end of the skewer in the modeling clay. Tilt the skewer so that it is at a slight angle. This represents the tilt of Earth's axis.

**3** Darken the room and turn on the lamp. Slowly rotate the skewer so that the dots on the ball move in and out of the light.

## Look and Discover

- **What happened when you rotated the ball? How much of the ball did the light shine on at one time? How many dots were in the light at one time?**

Like the ball on the skewer, Earth rotates on an invisible, tilted axis as it revolves around the Sun. When the ball spins, different sides move into and out of the light. Earth does the same on its axis. One side of it faces the Sun as the other side faces away. This means that when it is day in some parts of the world, it is night in others.

# The Changing Seasons

This simple activity can show you how the seasons change as Earth, rotating on its tilted axis, travels around the Sun. You'll be able to see how the length of daylight and nighttime change according to the season.

## Materials
- a lamp with no shade
- masking tape
- a pen
- a globe on a stand
- modeling clay

## Procedure

**1** Place the lamp on a table. Use pieces of the masking tape and a pen to mark four positions around the lamp at right angles to each other and about 3 feet from the lamp. Label the tape pieces *March*, *June*, *September*, and *December*.

**2** Place the globe at the December position. Put books underneath it until its top is level with the top of the lamp bulb. Fasten small balls of clay to the globe at the equator, the North Pole, the South Pole, halfway between the equator and the North Pole, and halfway between the equator and the South Pole.

**3** Point the South Pole of the globe toward the bulb (the Sun). This is approximately the position of Earth and the Sun in the month of December.

22

**4** Darken the room and turn on the lamp. Rotate the globe slowly counterclockwise. One complete rotation represents 24 hours. When the clay is lit by the lamp, that part of Earth is experiencing day. When the clay is in **shadow**, it is night.

**5** Repeat Steps 1 to 4 with the globe at the March, June, and September positions. Keep the North Pole of Earth's axis pointing in the same direction as you move the globe around the lamp. In the June position, the North Pole will tilt toward the Sun.

## The Equinoxes and the Solstices

**Equinoxes** occur twice each year. These are the two days on which the Sun is directly overhead at noon on the equator, and daylight hours equal darkness hours in both hemispheres. The summer and winter **solstices** are the two days with the longest and shortest amounts of daylight.

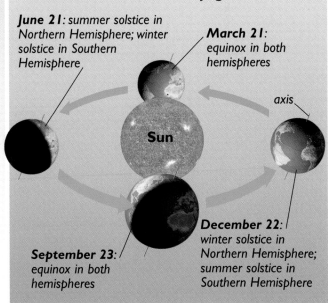

*June 21*: summer solstice in Northern Hemisphere; winter solstice in Southern Hemisphere

*March 21*: equinox in both hemispheres

*axis*

**Sun**

*September 23*: equinox in both hemispheres

*December 22*: winter solstice in Northern Hemisphere; summer solstice in Southern Hemisphere

## Look and Discover

- When you rotated the globe in the December position, how much daylight fell on the poles?
- How much light did the poles get at the March, June, and September positions? How much daylight did the equator get?

Because Earth's axis is tilted, parts of Earth get more daylight at different times of the year, and the Sun's rays hit different parts of Earth at different angles. This causes the varying lengths of day and night and the change in seasons.

# Making a Sundial

Did you know that we can use the position of the Sun in the sky to help tell time? The following activity will help you make a clock called a **sundial**, to tell time on sunny days. Remember that it's dangerous to look directly at the Sun. Use the angle of shadows to tell time.

**!** Ask an adult to help you with Step 2.

## Materials
- a piece of cardboard
- a drawing compass
- scissors
- a flowerpot
- a sharp pencil
- modeling clay
- glue

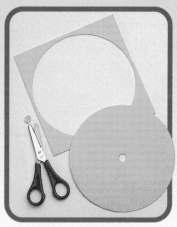

## Procedure

**1** Draw a large circle on the cardboard, using the compass.

**2** Cut out the circle and make a small hole in the center.

**3** Push the point of the pencil through the hole in the bottom of the flowerpot. Use the clay to hold the pencil in place.

24

**4** Turn the pot over so that the pencil is sticking out. Put the cardboard circle over the pencil and glue it to the bottom of the flowerpot.

**5** Set the flowerpot outside on a sunny morning. Every hour on the hour, draw around the shadow of the pencil on the card. Write the time next to each mark. Don't move the sundial.

**6** Look at the sundial again on the next sunny day. Make sure it has not moved from its position. (If it rains before the next sunny day, cover the sundial loosely with plastic.)

## Look and Discover

- **When you looked at the sundial again, did the pencil's shadow point to the correct time? Explain what happened.**

The rotation of Earth on its axis makes the Sun appear to move across the sky from east to west every day. The shadows cast by the Sun also appear to move. On sunny days, these shadows can be used to tell time, since the shadows will be cast in almost the same position at the same time each day.

## Shadows

When light strikes an opaque object, the light is blocked, creating a shadow. Most shadows are made up of a darker area and a lighter area. The darker area of a shadow, where all the light is blocked, is called the umbra. The lighter part is called the penumbra. In this area, only part of the light is blocked.

With the light behind him and low in the sky, the boy casts a long shadow.

# The Moon

Reflected sunlight gives the Moon its brightness. The same side of the Moon is always facing Earth. This is because the Moon rotates only once during its month-long **orbit** around Earth. Though the far side of the Moon is sometimes called the "dark side," it isn't really dark. It experiences sunshine and darkness, just as the near side of the Moon does—we just can't see that from Earth. The activities in this chapter will help you explore how the Moon's motion changes the way it looks to us.

## The Moon's Phases

Complete this activity with a friend to see how the Moon appears from Earth. You can also visualize how Earth and the Moon appear from space.

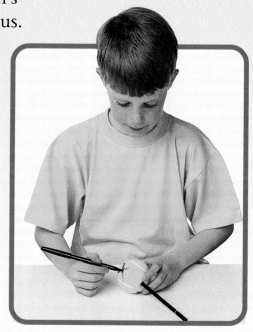

**!** Ask an adult to help you with Step 1.

### Materials
- a pencil
- a tennis ball
- a pen
- a desk lamp

### Procedure

**1** Ask an adult to stick a pencil into the tennis ball. A hole can be made first with an awl or other sharp object, such as a screwdriver. The ball will be your Moon. Mark one side of the ball with an *X* and the other side with a dark spot.

**2** Turn off any overhead lights and turn on the lamp. Stand in front of the lamp, holding the tennis ball with the dark spot facing you. You will be "on Earth." Have a friend stand nearby. Your friend will observe you "from space."

**3** Keep the tennis ball out in front of you while you slowly turn around in a circle, making sure that your body doesn't block light from the lamp. Look at the ball as you turn.

## Look and Discover

• **As you rotated slowly, how much of the ball could you see? How did the ball's appearance change?**
• **What did your friend see?**

The Moon circles Earth about once a month. As it moves, its **phase** changes. The phase is the amount of the lighted part of the Moon's surface that can be seen from Earth. As you slowly turn, you will see phases of the Moon. As you turned, you viewed the Moon as it looks from Earth. Your friend viewed how Earth and the Moon look from space.

## A Lunar Month

The period from one new Moon to the next is known as a "lunar month." Many ancient cultures used the lunar month as a basis for their calendars, as do some cultures today. However, twelve lunar months do not make a full year. So, as time passes, important holidays based on a lunar calendar can change dates.

# A Lunar Eclipse

Two or three times a year, a strange sight appears in the night sky. The Moon is wholly or partly covered by a shadow. This is called a **lunar eclipse**. An almanac can tell you when a lunar eclipse is due. Meanwhile, complete the activity to create your own lunar eclipse.

> ⚠ **Ask an adult to help you with Step 1.**

## Materials
- 2 thin wooden skewers, each about 10 inches long
- a ball 3 inches in diameter
- a ball 1½ inches in diameter
- modeling clay
- a 4-by-24-inch sheet of cardboard
- a desk lamp

## Procedure

**1** Have an adult push a skewer into each ball. Use the clay to stand the skewers up at either end of the cardboard. Make the centers of the balls the same height. The large ball represents Earth, and the small ball represents the Moon.

**2** Position the lamp—which represents the Sun—at the same height as Earth, but on the opposite side of Earth from the Moon. Shine the light directly at Earth. Then move the cardboard a small amount from side to side.

*Earth blocks light from the Sun, casting a shadow over the Moon.*

28

## Look and Discover

- What happened to the Moon when you moved the cardboard? Where did Earth cast a shadow?

Lunar eclipses occur when the Moon is in Earth's shadow. This happens when Earth sits exactly between the Sun and the Moon. The movement of the cardboard shows how the Moon moves into Earth's shadow and out again.

## Lunar Eclipse

Lunar eclipses occur only during a full Moon. During a total lunar eclipse, the entire Moon passes through Earth's shadow. It may disappear from view or be visible as a reddish disk. A partial eclipse occurs when only part of the Moon passes through Earth's shadow.

# Conclusion

Light plays an important role in the lives of all living things. Through these activities, you have explored the different ways light behaves, inventions created to study or use light, and how light influences day and night, the seasons, and the brightness of the Moon. Continue to explore and experiment with light. Discover all the exciting ways that light affects the world you live in.

# Glossary

**axis**
the imaginary line through the center of Earth, around which Earth rotates

**equinoxes**
the two days of the year when the Sun is directly overhead at the equator at noon, and day and night are equal in length

**incandescent**
emitting light as a result of being heated

**light rays**
straight beams of light

**lunar eclipse**
a time when Earth is directly between the Sun and the Moon, and part or all of the Moon passes partially or totally into Earth's shadow

**opaque**
not letting light pass through

**orbit**
the motion of one object in space around another, such as Earth around the Sun or the Moon around Earth

**periscope**
an instrument used to view objects that may be hidden by an obstacle

**phase**
the lighted part of the Moon's surface that can be seen from Earth

**prisms**
triangular blocks of glass or transparent plastic used to refract light

**reflection**
the bouncing of light waves from a surface

**refraction**   the change in direction of light rays as they pass from one medium into another

**shadow**   area of darkness produced when light is blocked by an opaque object

**solstices**   the two days in a year when the Sun is farthest from the equator at noon

**spectroscope**   an instrument that separates a beam of light into a spectrum showing all the different colors that the light contains

**sundial**   an instrument that uses a shadow to indicate time of day

**translucent**   allowing some light to pass through, scattering rays in the process

**transparent**   allowing most light to pass through without scattering it

**visible spectrum**   the range of colors produced by all wavelengths in white light

**wavelength**   the distance from one crest to the next crest in a wave; for visible light, different wavelengths correspond to different colors

# Index